the promise of Mothers
and
Daughters

SOURCEBOOKS, INC.®
NAPERVILLE, ILLINOIS

Compiled and written by Susan Yoder Benton

Published by Sourcebooks, Inc.
P.O. Box 4410, Naperville, Illinois 60567-4410
(630) 961-3900
FAX: (630) 961-2168
www.sourcebooks.com
ISBN 1-4022-0062-5

Printed and bound in the United States of America
IN 10 9 8 7 6 5 4 3 2 1

What do girls do who haven't any mothers to help them through their troubles?

—Louisa May Alcott

treetalk and windsong are

the language of my mother

her music does not leave me.

—Barbara Mahone

MOTHERS AND DAUGHTERS

Now I am nothing but a veil; all my body is a veil beneath which a child sleeps.

—Gabriela Mistral

Children love to hear the stories of their births. My mother always said giving birth to me was a wonderful experience, and I believe that has colored my self-image from the start.

Bringing a child

into the world is

the greatest act

of hope there is.

—Louise Hart

Little wild baby, that knowest not
where thou art going,
Lie still! Thy mother will do the rowing.

—Margaret Thomson Janvier

Before my daughter was born,
I thought of motherhood as a
single thing. But I find I am
transformed continually as the
mother of a baby becomes the
mother of a toddler, then a
pre-teen and so on. It's
a new job every day.

Walk heavily as a wheat stalk
at its full time bending towards
the earth waiting for the reaper.
Let your life swell downward
so you become like a vase, a
vessel. Let the unknown child
knock and knock against you
and rise like a dolphin within.

—Meridel Le Sueur

Like a new lover, I celebrated
every inch of her: every facial
expression, her radiant eyes,
her tiny fingers, her movements,
and her smile. Oh, that baby smile!

—Alexandra Stoddard

When my baby says "Mama,"
it is in a tone of discovery and
comfort, knowing that with a
simple vocalization she is connected
to the center of her universe.

—Megan Northland

What feeling in all the world
is so nice as that of a
child's hand in yours? It
is soft. It is small and
warm. It is as innocent
and guileless as a rabbit
or a puppy or a kitten
huddling in the shelter
of your clasp.

—Marjorie Holmes

12

I was awe-struck by the responsibility of raising a daughter. As she grew, I looked for signs that those mistakes I made during the first six months would come back to haunt me. Fortunately, by the time she was two I was sufficiently impressed by her resilience to lighten up.

13

MOTHERS
AND DAUGHTERS

Like a round loaf...
I kneaded you, patted you,
greased you smooth,
floured you.

—Judit Tóth

I feel things on a deeper level.
I have a kind of understanding about
my body, about being a woman.

—Shelley Long

How pleasant
it is to see
a human
countenance
that cannot
be insincere!

—Sophia A. Hawthorne

There was a little girl
Who had a little curl right in
the middle of her forehead,
When she was good she was
very, very good, but when she
was bad she was horrid.

—Henry Wadsworth Longfellow

Few things
are more rewarding
than a child's
open uncalculating
devotion.

—Vera Brittain

Although I'm still exhausted at day's end, I'm intensely in love with my daughter and declare her the most beautiful baby ever born.

—April Burk

Who, but a mother,
lies awake at night feeling
her daughter's pain?

—Carol T. Jacobson

Being a mother brings the
whole world into sharp focus.
Suddenly, everything that
happens is critical because
of how it may affect
my daughter's life.

My daughter pretty much hit the ground running at age one, and she's been on the move ever since. Thank goodness for cell phones — now she gives me a running commentary on her life as she moves from home to car to job and back.

MOTHERS AND DAUGHTERS

It takes hard work and hard thinking to rear good people. The job is interesting, although the hours are bad, starting from the first day.

—Marguerite Kelly and Elia Parsons

I watch my little girl
at play, all innocence
and forgetfulness, a new
beginning, perpetual motion,
daughter of life.

I loved the first six months of her life because I would just roll her up in a blanket, and she'd lie there on the bed and look at me. And I would just write and I was very happy.

—Mary Morris

What a difference it makes to come home to a child!

—Margaret Fuller

I was so surprised when I first saw my daughter. We had been so intimate when she was still inside me—once she was born, it was like meeting a pen pal or someone you'd had long phone conversations with but never seen.

Suddenly, through birthing
a daughter, a woman finds herself
face to face not only with an
infant, a little girl, a woman-
to-be, but also with her own
unresolved conflicts from the
past and her hopes and
dreams for the future.

—Elizabeth Debold

I gave birth to her,
I nourish her, and still
I don't own her, I don't
rule her—this is how
it should be.

It's blissful if I can sleep
beside my three-year-old
daughter and begin waking up,
oh say, fifteen minutes before
she does. Ah yes, ecstasy.

—Penny Reid

My mother believed in my beauty and talent even through the ugly, awkward years—I clung to her faith in me until I could have faith in myself.

When people ask me
what I do, I always say
I am a mother first.
Your children represent
your thoughts.
Your children are
a statement.

—Jacqueline Jackson

MOTHERS
AND DAUGHTERS

The knowingness
of little girls
Is hidden underneath
their curls.

—Phyllis McGinley

No song or poem will bear my mother's name. Yet so many of the stories that I write, that we all write, are my mother's stories.

—Alice Walker

As my daughter grows,
I see in her developing
features the
faces of my
mother, and my
grandmother,
and a kaleidoscope
of her ancestors,
all melding into
a new face that's
uniquely her own.

And women know that
once you become pregnant and
have a child, you have the
opportunity to become closer
to your mother than ever before,
closer to your sister and your
aunts, closer to elderly neighbors
who have had children.

—Linda Vallejo

Talking, they combed
our hair, rocked us
to sleep, sang to us,
told us tales of then
and now—and tomorrow.
They worried about us.
They hoped for us and
showed us the way.

—Virginia Hamilton

Your mother is your hero, your nemesis, your best friend, and your worst critic, all wrapped up in one smiling package.

My mother was my
first jealous lover.

—Barbara Grizzuti Harrison

Who ran to help me when I fell,

And would some pretty story tell,

Or kiss the place to make it well?

My Mother.

—Ann Taylor

I cannot forget my mother.
Though not as sturdy as
others, she is my bridge.
When I needed to get across,
she steadied herself long
enough for me to run
across safely.

—Renita Weems

MOTHERS
AND DAUGHTERS

I love to go home and cook a holiday meal with my mother. We are so used to each other around the kitchen. I'll flip what's in her skillet and she'll stir what's in my pot, like we were one grand cook with four arms and hands.

My mother, religious-negro, proud of

having waded through a storm, is very obviously,

a sturdy Black bridge that I

crossed over, on.

—Carolyn M. Rodgers

A mother...is forever surprised and even faintly wronged that her sons and daughters are just people, for many mothers hope and half expect that their newborn child will make the world better, will somehow be a redeemer. Perhaps they are right, and they can believe that the rare quality they glimpsed in the child is active in the burdened adult.

—Florida Scott-Maxwell

A good mother expects your best, and gives you her best, without demanding perfection from either of you.

My mother researched our
family's genealogy. There they
are: the names, the significant dates
(birth, marriage, children, death),
sometimes with faded
photographs, the lives that
somehow made
me possible.

I wonder why you care so much about me—no, I don't wonder. I only accept it as the thing at the back of all one's life that makes everything bearable and possible.

—Gertrude Bell

When I told my mother I was going to be a millionaire when I grew up, she didn't ask "How are you going to make all that money?" She said, "How wonderful! What will you do with all that money?"

54

To her whose heart is my heart's
quiet home, To my first Love,
my Mother, on whose knee I learnt
love-lore that is not troublesome.

—Christina Rossetti

My mother was so much a child herself—small and delicate, but adventurous and fun-loving—that she made my childhood a delight.

Nothing was as
beautiful as the sound
of my mother's voice
singing to me
at bedtime.
Nothing so sweet,
so soothing, so right.

MOTHERS
AND DAUGHTERS

I want to lean into
her the way wheat
leans into wind.

—Louise Erdrich

i am not you anymore
i am my own collection of
gifts and errors.
—Saundra Sharp

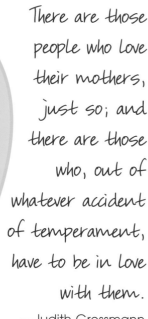

There are those
people who love
their mothers,
just so; and
there are those
who, out of
whatever accident
of temperament,
have to be in love
with them.

—Judith Grossmann

We don't speak at night anymore, but she's left me her legacy nonetheless—a love for the sea and the smoothness of pearls, an appreciation of music and words, sympathy for the underdog, and a disregard for boundaries.

—Cristina Garcia

Surely it's some kind of cosmic joke when you, your visiting mother, and your teenage daughter all have PMS together.

And it came to me, and
I knew what I had to have
before my soul would
rest. I wanted to
belong—to belong to my
mother. And in return—I
wanted my mother to
belong to me.

—Gloria Vanderbilt

I sharpen more
and more to your
Likeness every year.

—Michele Wolf

My mother seemed always
to be concerned with getting
dinner, or feeding the cat, or
paying the bills, but somehow,
between the trivial things, she
taught me about listening
with compassion, about growing
spiritually, about taking
care of the world.

My mother allows me the luxury of getting mad at her, because we both know that I could never get mad enough to burn off any of the love between us. She allows herself the same luxury.

MOTHERS
AND DAUGHTERS

A woman is her mother.
That's the main thing.

—Anne Sexton

My mom is the only person I know who is more sarcastic than I am. When we get together we have to talk in double negatives to communicate at all.

In search of my
mother's garden,
I found my own.

—Alice Walker

Mother, in ways neither of us
can ever understand,
I have come home.
—Robin Morgan

My mother is the only person I know with whom I can resume a conversation exactly where it left off, whether yesterday or six months ago.

If daughters absorb the messages of their mother's lives, they at some point step off course, jettisoning some things, choosing...others, then making up the rest as they go along...

—Lauren Cowen and Jayne Wexler

My mother is a poem
I'll never be able to write
though everything I write is
a poem to my mother.

—Sharon Doubiago

My mother remembers
my childhood through
rose-colored glasses.

If you've ever had a mother and she's given you and meant to you all the things you care for most, you never get over it.

—Anne Douglas Sedgwick

I learned your walk, talk, gestures and nurturing laughter. At that time, Mama, had you swung from bars, I would, to this day, be hopelessly, imitatively, hung up.

—Diane Bogus

MOTHERS
AND DAUGHTERS

My mother
is my hero.

'Twas her thinking of others
that made you think of her.

—Elizabeth Barrett Browning

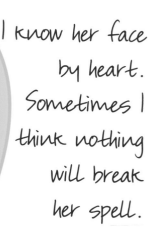

I know her face
by heart.
Sometimes I
think nothing
will break
her spell.

—Daphne Merkin

When my mother was sick,
I had the wonderful
opportunity to take
care of her the way she
had cared for me when
I was little. The first
thing I did was to make
chicken soup, of course.

You never get over
bein' a child long's
you have a mother
to go to.

—Sarah Orne Jewett

I am a reflection of
my mother's secret
poetry as well as of
her hidden angers.

—Audre Lorde

Mothers and daughters
don't always get along, but they'll
always love each other.

Most of all the other beautiful things in life come by twos and threes, by dozens and hundreds. Plenty of roses, stars, sunsets, rainbows, brothers and sisters, aunts and cousins, comrades and friends—but only one mother in the whole world.

—Kate Douglas Wiggin

Yes, Mother...I can
see you are flawed.
You have not hidden it.
That is your greatest
gift to me.

—Alice Walker

MOTHERS
AND DAUGHTERS

It's all right for a woman
to be, above all, human.

—Anaïs Nin

After my daughter was born, and the reality of motherhood and career set in, I called my mother and said, "How did you do it?" Of course, she couldn't tell me.

No matter how old a mother is she watches her middle-aged children for signs of improvement.

—Florida Scott-Maxwell

My mother never
listens to me.

—Marjorie Weinman Sharmat

Mothers...are basically a patient lot. They have to be or they would devour their offspring early on, like guppies.

—Mary Daheim

Mothers had a thousand
thoughts to get through
within a day, and...most
of these were about
avoiding disaster.

—Natalie Kusz

If my teenage daughter is only half as wild as I was at her age, it will still be enough to drive me crazy.

Mother who gave me life
I think of women bearing
women. Forgive me the wisdom
I would not learn from you.

—Gwen Harwood

Oh, if only I could spare my daughter my mistakes! It wrenches my heart that some things she can only learn by experience.

Now that I am in my forties...we have the long, personal and even remarkably honest phone calls I always wanted so intensely I forbade myself to imagine them. How strange...I am deeply grateful. With my poems, I finally won even my mother. The longest wooing of my life.

—Marge Piercy

MOTHERS
AND DAUGHTERS

I...have another cup of coffee with my mother. We get along very well, veterans of a guerrilla war we never understood.

—Joan Didion

My daughter asks, "Why is
grandma so nice and you're so mean?"
I sigh. "She doesn't have to raise
you. Her job is done."

A mother's hardest
to forgive.
Life is the fruit
she longs to
hand you,
Ripe on a plate.
And while you live,
Relentlessly she
understands you.

—Phyllis McGinley

There is a stage with people we love when we are no longer separate from them, but so close in sympathy that we live through them as directly as through ourselves.... We push back our hair because theirs is in their eyes.

—Nan Fairbrother

Sometimes lately I
look at my writing as
it leaves the pen and
get the spooky sensation
that my mother is
writing it — has my
handwriting always
looked so much
like hers?

I fear, as any daughter would, losing myself back into the mother.

—Kim Chernin

Why should I
be reasonable?
I'm your mother.

—Lynne Alpern and Esther Blumenfeld

My mother phones daily to ask, "Did you just try to reach me?" When I reply, "No," she adds, "So, if you're not too busy, call me while I'm still alive," and hangs up.

—Erma Bombeck

My mother has a curious shyness about our relationship; whenever I call she says she was just wishing she could talk to me—but she waits for me to call. It's as though she wants reassurance, each time, that I'm really interested.

MOTHERS AND DAUGHTERS

Did you ever meet a mother who's complained that her child phoned her too often? Me neither.

—Maureen Lipman

I thought the greatest challenges of motherhood would be facing the deep spiritual or emotional issues of life with my children, but it's keeping track of my daughter's backpack and mittens that seems to be beyond me.

My mother is a
woman who speaks
with her life as much
as with her tongue.

—Kesaya E. Noda

She knew how to make virtues out of necessities.

—Audre Lorde

Even in silence, she gives me the confidence to do what I believe is right, to trust my own perceptions.

—Cristina Garcia

I was almost a teenager before I realized that not everyone's mother worked outside the home. Mom felt guilty sometimes but what she gave me is a role model who lives a life she loves.

My mother arrived the day
after my daughter was born.
Seeing her toss that newborn over
one shoulder and carry on with
laundry was a revelation to me.
I was so new to mothering—
I thought the baby would break.

To describe my mother
would be to write about
a hurricane in its
perfect power.

—Maya Angelou

121

When the strongest words for
what I have to offer come out
of me sounding like words
I remember from my
mother's mouth, then I
either have to reassess the
meaning of everything I have
to say now, or re-examine
the worth of her old words.

—Audre Lorde

After I had my daughter
I was struck by a profound
understanding of what my
mother went through.
I called to thank her —
she laughed! I look
forward to that
conversation with
my own daughter.

MOTHERS
AND DAUGHTERS

A mother is not a person
to lean upon, but a person to
make leaning unnecessary.

—Dorothy Canfield

...her smile was like a rainbow
after a sudden storm.

—Colette

No one can make me as furious as my mother, probably because I know how well she knows me. I can't pretend with her and that's what makes me mad.

She said that if I listened to her, later I would know what she knew: where true words came from, always from up high, above everything else. And if I didn't listen to her, she said my ear would bend too easily to other people, all saying words that had no lasting meaning, because they came from the bottom of their hearts, where their own desires lived, a place where I could not belong.

—Amy Tan

If I can be half
as generous with
my daughter as
my mother has
been with me, I'll
be very happy.

Only a
mother
knows a
mother's
fondness.

—Lady Mary Wortley
Montagu

Pregnancy doubled her, birth halved her, and motherhood turned her into Everywoman.

—Erica Jong

At that moment, I missed
my mother more than I had
ever imagined possible and wanted
only to live somewhere quiet and
beautiful with her alone, but also
at that moment I wanted only
to see her lying dead, all withered
and in a coffin at my feet.

—Jamaica Kincaid

She did not understand
how her father could have
reached such age and such
eminence without learning that
all mothers are as infallible
as any pope and more
righteous than any saint.

—Frances Newman

134

MOTHERS AND DAUGHTERS

My mother taught me there was nothing I couldn't do if I set my mind to it. What a wonderful legacy to pass on to my daughter.

A mother's love for her child is like nothing else in the world. It knows no law, no pity, it dares all things and crushes down remorselessly all that stands in its path.

—Agatha Christie

She had risen and was walking about the room, her fat, worn face sharpening with a sort of animal alertness into power and protection. The claws that hide in every maternal creature slipped out of the fur of good manners.

—Margaret Deland

Motherhood is like Albania—
you can't trust the descriptions
in the books, you have to go there.

—Marni Jackson

I cringe when my daughter suffers the cruelties and confusions of childhood friendships; I remember them well. I can't shield her from all pain; but I am there to help her cope, as my mother was there for me.

There is no other closeness
in human life like the closeness
between a mother and her
baby—chronologically, physically,
and spiritually they are just
a few heartbeats away from
being the same person.

—Susan Cheever

My mother always found me out.
Always. She's been dead for
thirty-five years, but I have
this feeling that even now
she's watching.

—Natalie Babbitt

I want to raise my daughter differently from the way my mother raised me, but I want her to turn out just like me.

My mother wasn't what the world would call a good woman. She never said she was. And many people, including the police, said she was a bad woman. But she never agreed with them, and she had a way of lifting up her head when she talked back to them that made me know she was right.

—Box-Car Bertha

The most important thing she'd learned over the years was that there was no way to be a perfect mother and a million ways to be a good one.

—Jill Churchill

MOTHERS
AND DAUGHTERS

The miracle of birth
is nothing to the miracle
of getting kids out the door
on time for school.

I became a new person when
I became a mother. I could
not have imagined it.

You might not have thought it possible to give birth to others before one has given birth to oneself, but I assure you it is quite possible. It has been done; I offer myself in evidence as Exhibit A.

—Sheila Ballantyne

I never would have gotten an A in high school trigonometry if my mother hadn't tutored me. She actually made math fun at a time when all I could think about was boys. That takes real character and imagination.

A mother always has to think twice, once for herself and once for her child.

—Sophia Loren

Over the years I
have learned that
motherhood is much like
an austere religious
order, the joining of
which obligates one to
relinquish all claims to
personal possessions.

—Nancy Stahl

My daughter
is my mother's
revenge.

My mother was a genius.
None of my friend's mothers
could recite "The Owl and
the Pussycat" from
memory, and certainly
not with such flair.

When her biographer says
of an Italian woman poet,
"during some years her Muse
was intermitted," we do not
wonder at the fact when
he casually mentions
her ten children.

—Anna Garlin Spencer

MOTHERS
AND DAUGHTERS

Being asked to decide between your passion for work and your passion for children was like being asked by your doctor whether you preferred him to remove your brain or your heart.

—Mary Kay Blakely

Most mothers entering the labor market outside the home are naive. They stagger home each evening, holding mail in their teeth, the cleaning over their arm, a lamb chop defrosting under each armpit, balancing two gallons of frozen milk between their knees, and expect one of the kids to get the door.

—Erma Bombeck

At work, you think of the children you've left at home. At home, you think of the work you've left unfinished. Such a struggle is unleashed within yourself: your heart is rent.

—Golda Meir

When I call home and my daughter answers the phone, it's like hearing my own voice say hello.

My mother taught me to balance a checkbook and balance on high heels, to change the oil in the car and change my makeup to suit my mood, to read the mood of a committee and the mood of a date, to make a killing in the marketplace and a killing on the dance floor.

There is only one image in this culture of the "good mother"...She is quietly strong, selflessly giving, undemanding, unambitious; she is receptive and intelligent in only a moderate, concrete way; she is of even temperament, almost always in control of her emotions. She loves her children completely and unambivalently. Most of us are not like her.

—Jane Lazarre

My daughter tried to fire
me from my position as
mother. She said my job
performance was shaky. I said
you couldn't fire a volunteer.

When I had my daughter,
I learned what the sound of one
hand clapping is—it's a woman
holding an infant in one arm
and a pen in the other.

—Kate Braverman

Reminds me of what
one of mine wrote in a
third-grade piece on how
her mother spent her
time. She reported
"one half time on
home, one half time on
outside things, one half
time writing."

—Charlotte Montgomery

Nothing else ever will make you as happy or as sad, as proud or as tired, for nothing is quite as hard as helping a person develop his own individuality—especially while you struggle to keep your own.

—Marguerite Kelly and Elia Parsons

MOTHERS
AND DAUGHTERS

Cleaning your house while your kids are still growing Is like shoveling the walk before it stops snowing.

—Phyllis Diller

Being a daughter is only half the equation; bearing one is the other.

—Erica Jong

As the mother talks, she strokes her daughter's hair. As the daughter talks, she rubs her mother's back, smoothes her blouse. Loving mothers and daughters simply could not keep their hands off one another.

—Carol Saline

My ideal day would be to drop my daughter off at school at eight-thirty, sit down at my desk, and then at two-thirty go to the gym and swim, do my errands, and pick her up after school. But I almost never have a day like that.

—Mary Morris

I can't explain how I know when my mother is thinking about me, but I do. At least, whenever I get that feeling and call her, she says, "I was just thinking about you."

The woman who bore
me is no longer
alive, but I seem
to be her daughter
in increasingly
profound ways.

—Johnetta B. Cole

Making the decision to have a child—it's momentous. It is to decide forever to have your heart go walking around outside your body.

—Elizabeth Stone

As though experiencing
an earthquake, mothers
of daughters may find their
lives shifted, their deep
feelings unearthed, the
balance struck in all
relationships once
again off kilter.

—Elizabeth Debold

All daughters, even when most aggravated by their mothers, have a secret respect for them. They believe perhaps that they can do everything better than their mothers can, and many things they can do better, but they have not yet lived long enough to be sure how successfully they will meet the major emergencies of life, which lie, sometimes quite creditably, behind their mothers.

—Phyllis Bottome

MOTHERS AND DAUGHTERS

Maybe life would have been easier if I hadn't had my daughter. Maybe it would have been less stressful, or less busy. All I know is that when she came into my life, it was as though my life had finally begun. What had I been doing all those years that had seemed so important?

My mother taught me how
to do everything—how to plant
pansies, how to make piecrust,
how to refinish furniture, how to
hem a skirt, how to work crossword
puzzles, how to write term papers,
how to talk to people. How could
I have survived without her?

It seems to me that since I've had children, I've grown richer and deeper. They may have slowed down my writing for a while, but when I did write, I had more of a self to speak from.

—Anne Tyler

One thing all women
have in common is that
we are all daughters.

Seeing my mother and my daughter together reminds me of basking in the love of my own grandmother. Of course, the two them want to be left alone; they don't want me around to spoil the fun.

Children use up
the same part of my
head as poetry does.
To deal with children is
a matter of terrific
imaginative identification.

—Libby Houston

My children...have been
a constant joy to me
(except on the days
when they weren't).

—Evelyn Fairbanks

When my daughter had her ears pierced, it was earth shattering—imagine purposely piercing that perfect skin.

It kills you to
see them grow up.
But I guess
it would kill
you quicker if
they didn't.

—Barbara Kingsolver

Adorable children
are considered to
be the general
property of the
human race. (Rude
children belong to
their mothers.)

—Judith Martin (Miss Manners)

MOTHERS AND DAUGHTERS

Too much indulgence
has ruined thousands
of children; too much
Love not one.

—Fanny Fern

We love those we feed, not vice
versa; in caring for others we
nourish our own self-esteem.

—Jessamyn West

Just for a little while, they believe in the perfect mom—that is, you, whoever and wherever you happen to be.

—Anna Quindlen

194

My mother taught
me to speak up for
myself. It was a hard
transition, because it
was so comforting to
let her speak for me.

Likely as not, the
child you can do
the least with will
do the most to
make you proud.

—Mignon McLaughlin

As the youngsters
grow attached to
their teachers and
classmates...they can
finally say goodbye to
their mothers without
re-enacting the death
scene from Camille.

—Sue Mittenthal

Mom was brilliant at encouraging my creativity. I never knew my limits; I could explore the fantastic landscape of my imagination without any thought of censorship.

My daughter already
has many talents I don't-
she can sing, she can play a
musical instrument. It's
so true that we want our
kids to exceed our own
accomplishments.

Life with a daughter of nine
through twelve is a special experience
for parents, particularly mothers.
In a daughter's looks, actions,
attitudes, passions, loves, and hates,
in her fears and her foibles, a mother
will see herself at the same age.
You are far enough away to have some
perspective on what your daughter is
going through. Still, you are close enough,
if reminded, to feel it all again.

—Stella Chess

MOTHERS
AND DAUGHTERS

A daughter is a mother's gender partner,
her closest ally in the family confederacy,
an extension of her self. And mothers
are their daughters' role model, their
biological and emotional road map,
the arbiter of all their relationships.

—Victoria Secunda

My daughter, at eleven

(almost twelve), is like a garden.

Oh, darling! Born in that sweet birthday suit

and having owned it and known it for so long,

now you must watch high noon enter...

—Anne Sexton

Sometimes I look at my eleven-year-old daughter and I can see her when she was one and I can see what her face will look like when she's twenty-one.

What the daughter does,
the mother did.

—Jewish Proverb

I was about sixteen
when I finally started
to understand that my
mother's anger and her
fears for me were one
and the same.

When a mother quarrels with
a daughter, she has a double dose
of unhappiness—hers from the
conflict, and empathy with her
daughter's from the conflict with
her. Throughout her life a mother
retains this special need to
maintain a good relationship
with her daughter.

—Terri Apter

I shall be glad to see
thee back, daughter, for
I miss thee dreadfully.

—Hannah Whitall Smith

I could never stay
angry with my mother;
it made me miserable.
And she was always so
ready to make up.

When you were born
I held you wet and
unfolding, like a
butterfly newly
born from the
chrysalis of my body.

—Joy Harjo

What bliss it was to have a little girl! A doll to dress, a cherub to cuddle, a girl to commiserate with, a sharp mind to teach, a friend to trust, a beauty to be proud of.

MOTHERS
AND DAUGHTERS

I have a photograph of my mother, my daughter, and me—a prized possession. We all have the same eyebrows!

nine months passed and my body
heavy with the knowledge of gods
turned landward, came to rest.

—Sonia Sanchez

As often as I
have witnessed the
miracle, held the
perfect creature
with its tiny
hands and feet,
each time I have
felt as though I
were entering a
cathedral with prayer
in my heart.

—Margaret Sanger

Unlike the mother-son relationship, a daughter's relationship with her mother is something akin to bungee diving. She can stake her claim in the outside world in what looks like total autonomy—in some cases, even "divorce" her mother in a fiery exit from the family—but there is an invisible emotional cord that snaps her back.

—Victoria Secunda

As is the
mother, so is
her daughter.

—Ezekiel 16:44

And thou
shalt in thy
daughter see,
This picture,
once, resembled
thee.

—Ambrose Philips

I do so many things
the way my mother did.
But she made it
look easy.

My Mamá Grande, a tiny Mayan woman, took me aside when I was an adolescent and told me several things that didn't make a bit of sense to my young and inattentive ears, and as young people tend to waste all attempts of our elders to relay to us wisdom accumulated over the decades, I thought my Mamá Grande had a few mice in the attic.

—Ana Castillo

My daughter and my mother have long cozy chats on the phone. Somehow they have a never-ending supply of things to talk about.

MOTHERS AND DAUGHTERS

We think back through our mothers if we are women.

—Virginia Woolf

...whatever else a woman may be, each and every one of us is a daughter.

—Carol Saline

My mother was reading to the baby to get her to take a nap. I was the one who fell asleep.

Our mothers and grandmothers,
some of them: moving to
music not yet written.

—Alice Walker

She said there were two
people you had to be true
to—those people who came
before you and those people
who came after you.

—Gayl Jones

The most important thing I learned from my mother was to take time for things like indoor picnics on rainy days, making collages, and as much cuddling as possible. You can go far on moments like those.

The art of mothering is handed down from one generation to the next.

—Wendy Jean Ruhl

Women had to stick together, mother, and protect each other. That was part of our culture.

—Willye White

I have a photo of my mother feeding my six-month-old daughter. There's food everywhere, including on the wall, and they're both grinning.

Women who outlive their daughters are orphans, Abuela tells me. Only their granddaughters can save them, guard their knowledge like the first fire.

—Cristina Garcia

MOTHERS
AND DAUGHTERS

What you teach your own children is what you really believe in.

—Cathy Warner Weatherford

Each generation supposes
that the world was simpler
for the one before it.

—Eleanor Roosevelt

Every generation must go further than the last or what's the use in it?

—Meridel le Sueur

My daughter listens to me about the same way I listened to my mother— with respectful disbelief, secure in the knowledge that I've never lived in her particular world.

Compassion for
our parents is
the true sign
of maturity.

—Anaïs Nin

I never quite realized how very young my mother was when she had me, until my daughter reached twenty-one.

We all carry the Houses
of our Youth inside, and our
Parents, too, grown small enough
to fit within our Hearts.

—Erica Jong

Generation after generation of women have pledged to raise their daughters differently, only to find that their daughters grow up and fervently pledge the same thing.

—Elizabeth Debold

We are never done with thinking about our parents, I suppose, and come to know them better long after they are dead than we ever did when they were alive.

—May Sarton

MOTHERS
AND DAUGHTERS

I couldn't be happy when my mother was sad or not feeling well. No matter the cause, I felt it was my job to cheer her up.

The debt of gratitude we
owe our mother and father goes
forward, not backward. What
we owe our parents is the
bill presented to us by
our children.

—Nancy Friday

Like father,
like son;
like mother,
like daughter.

—Chinese proverb

My mother says her
grandchildren are her dividends.

Kids don't stay with you if you do it right. It's one job where, the better you are, the more surely you won't be needed in the long run.

—Barbara Kingsolver

I cannot have a more
pleasing task than taking
care of my precious Child—
It is an amusement
to me preferable to
all others.

—Nancy Shippen Livingston

I birthed 'ya, I nursed 'ya, and
I wiped your bottom, girl—
that makes me your mama.

—Ma Yoder

I've learned a lot from my daughter about coping with life. She teaches me at least as much as I teach her.

I'll never forget
the day my daughter
stood up on her
own two feet—
"I am baby,
hear me roar!"

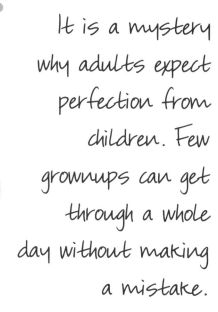

It is a mystery why adults expect perfection from children. Few grownups can get through a whole day without making a mistake.

—Marcelene Cox

MOTHERS
AND DAUGHTERS

Successful parenting was like log rolling, and she'd often landed in the drink.

—Lisa Alther

I knew I was both a blessing
and a bother to my mother,
as she was to me.

Admittedly, I was exhausted at times, but that didn't change the fact that I loved every minute that I shared with my daughters.

—Alexandra Stoddard

Like most other parents
I see my child through
an atmosphere which
illuminates, magnifies,
and at the same time
refines the object to
a degree that amounts
to a delusion.

—Sara Coleridge

I treat my daughter
differently when I
remember that she
is a future world
leader, and one day
her childhood will
be in her past.

If only we could
have them back as
babies today, now
that we have some
idea what to do
with them.

—Nancy Mairs

I occasionally wake up with a terrible pang and say, "I'm only going to have my daughter in the house for six more years."

—Mary Gordon

My mother has never
liked the places I've lived.
The only thing they had
in common was that
they were too far
away from home.

Seeing you sleeping on
your back among your stuffed
ducks, bears and basset
hounds would remind me
that no matter how good
the next day might be, certain
moments were gone forever....

—Joan Baez

MOTHERS AND DAUGHTERS

A mother develops a keen sense that tells her when her children are going to be hungry, or tired, or bored, before they know it themselves.

There are so many disciplines in being a parent besides the obvious ones like getting up in the night and putting up with the noise in the day. And almost the hardest of all is learning to be a well of affection and not a fountain, to show them we love them, not when we feel like it, but when they do.

—Nan Fairbrother

You can never
go home again,
but the truth is
you can never
leave home, so
it's all right.

—Maya Angelou

Time is the only comforter
for the loss of a mother.

—Jane Welsh Carlyle

My mother had all three of her children before she was twenty-four years old. She says it's best to have your children young, before you think about it too much, or you might lose your nerve.

When I go home, I stay in my
old room, where the desk still
holds photos of grade school
friends and the same books and
toys fill the shelves. I imagine
that any minute mom will
call me to supper and there
we will all be, as we were
twenty-five years ago.

My mom was great when I was upset. She knew when to listen attentively to my woes and when to just blow raspberries on my tummy.

Mama exhorted her children at every opportunity to "jump at [th]e sun." We might not land on the sun, but at least we would get off the ground.

—Zora Neale Hurston

Fortunately, my ideas about the role of a mother have changed a lot in the past eight years. I could never have survived my own perfectionism.

—Sheilah Marie Seaberg

I thought I wanted to know everything my daughter did until she reached about sixteen and still confided in me.

MOTHERS
AND DAUGHTERS

Each child has one extra line to your heart, which no other child can replace.

—Marguerite Kelly
and Elia Parsons

Mothers always know.

—Oprah Winfrey

Parents teach in the toughest school in the world—The School for Making People. You are the board of education, the principal, the classroom teacher, and the janitor.

—Virginia Satir

To have children is a double living, the earthly fountain of youth, a continual fresh delight, a volcano as well as a fountain, and also a source of weariness beyond description.

—Josephine W. Johnson

When I was about fourteen, I thought it highly perceptive of my mother to guess that when I got really quiet, it usually had to do with boys. It was new to me, and it didn't occur to me that she had ever gone through it herself.

Now that I'm a mother, and my mother is gone, I wish a hundred times a day that I could tell her, "I'm sorry, mom, now I understand."

Motherhood brings a feeling of being reunited. There can even be a kind of forgiveness of her own mother when she repeats with her daughter the very things she didn't like as a child.

—Nancy Friday

You are born to one mother,
but if you are lucky, you will have
more than one. And among them
all you will find most of what you
need. Your relationships with las todas
madres, the many mothers, will most
likely be ongoing ones, for the need
for guidance and advisement is
never outgrown, nor, from the
point of view of women's deep
creative life, should it ever be.

—Clarissa Pinkola Estés

I spent years trying to look perfect to my mother so she wouldn't be upset, and of course, I couldn't do it. Imagine my surprise when I realized she only wanted to be with me, and the only thing that really hurt her was my withholding myself.

MOTHERS
AND DAUGHTERS

Be the parent you wish you had and do it with love—love for your parents and love for your children.

—Paula Peisner Coxe

A lot of women told me it was liberating to realize they could act differently from mother and they wouldn't die. They could be themselves and mother still loved them. She didn't close the door and she didn't stop telephoning.

—Nancy Friday

As the years go by,
my mother and I relate on
many levels; sometimes
I feel I am mothering her,
and sometimes I feel
like a child in her presence.
Either way, there is a
timeless element of
nurturing that I think
is unique to mothers
and daughters.

The mark of a good parent is that she can have fun while being one.

—Marcelene Cox

I acknowledge the cold truth of her death for perhaps the first time. She is truly gone, forever out of reach, and I have become my own judge.

—Sheila Ballantyne

The mother to her daughter spake:

"Daughter," said she, "arise!

Thy daughter to her daughter take,

Whose daughter's daughter cries."

—Anonymous

My mother was a genius
at inexpensive entertainment—
if all else failed, she could
reduce us to a heap of giggles
by letting us bump down the
stairs on our rears.

What I would like to give my daughter is freedom.... Freedom is...not insisting that your daughter share your limitations. Freedom also means letting your daughter reject you when she needs to and come back when she needs to. Freedom is unconditional love.

—Erica Jong

Our house only had
one bathroom, and
I always followed my
mother into it, and
vice versa. We had
some of our best
conversations there,
which mystified my
dad and brothers.

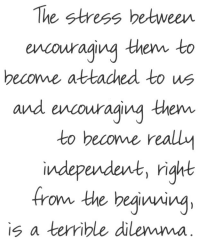

The stress between encouraging them to become attached to us and encouraging them to become really independent, right from the beginning, is a terrible dilemma.

—Dr. Sophie Freud

MOTHERS
AND DAUGHTERS

Daughter am I in my mother's house; But mistress in my own.

—Rudyard Kipling

When I heard my daughter's tiny three-year-old voice repeat a swear word I had used, that cured me of swearing!

Having children can smooth the relationship, too. Mother and daughter are now equals.

—Anna Quindlen

My great-grandfather used to say
to his wife, my great-grandmother,
who in turn told her daughter, my
grandmother, who repeated it to her
daughter, my mother, who used to
remind her daughter, my own sister,
that to talk well and eloquently
was a very great art, but that
an equally great one was to know
the right moment to stop.

—Wolfgang Amadeus Mozart

Growing up I thought my mother was great, but it's taken me years to appreciate how really talented she was, because she didn't know it herself.

306

As long as a
woman can look ten
years younger than
her own daughter,
she is perfectly
satisfied.

—Oscar Wilde

I love my mom. She's seventy-two years old and still inexpressibly cute.

My mother always says that she still feels seventeen inside. After looking at me, she is surprised by her own face in the mirror; the contrast between us seems incongruous.

My mother gives me lovely gifts — cashmere sweaters and silk teddies. I treasure them, even when the colors are more "her" than "me."

MOTHERS
AND DAUGHTERS

Of all the haunting moments
of motherhood, few rank with
hearing your own words come
out of your daughter's mouth.

—Victoria Secunda

The trick, which requires the combined skills of a tightrope walker and a cordon bleu chef frying a plain egg, is to take your [preteen] daughter seriously without taking everything she says and does every minute seriously.

—Stella Chess

I would sit on a stool in our tiny kitchen and pour out my heart to my mother as she cooked. Somehow a lot of teenage angst was baked, fried, stirred, and steamed out of existence.

The truth is that there is no perfection when it comes to parenting.

—Paula Peisner Coxe

Now that you are eighteen

I give you my booty, my spoils,

my Mother & Co. and

my ailments.

—Anne Sexton

Sexual activity, for women, has a history of vulnerability, in a way it simply does not have for men. The mother has to teach this hidden text to her daughter.

—Terri Apter

Early in my adolescence, my mother hit upon the happy cure of eating mint chocolate chip ice cream out of the carton with me. Barefoot on the bed, spoons in hand, the empathy in that gesture coaxed me out of the foulest moods imaginable.

Listening to learn from a daughter in adolescence, conspiring with her thoughts and feelings, keeps a mother in touch with a daughter's growing and changing self.

—Elizabeth Debold

A mid-life daughter may reengage with a mother or put new controls on care and set limits to love. But whatever she does, her child's history is never finished.

—Terri Apter

How can a girl who spends hours on e-Bay hunting down bargains with the finely honed instincts of a predator not have time to sew on a button?

MOTHERS
AND DAUGHTERS

Girls learn what
it is to be a woman by
watching women.

—Sondra Forsyth

My mother never laughed at
my fashion crises, even when I was
in eighth grade and thought
magenta hair was a good idea.

I'm real playful with it, that's one thing. Being a mother just balances me out as a human being so that I can do my work.

—Linda Vallejo

Most parents of adolescent girls have the goal of keeping their daughters safe while they grow up and explore the world. The parents' job is to protect, the daughter's job is to explore.

—Mary Pipher

I was pleased
that my daughter
seemed to be
getting into arts
and crafts, until I
realized that didn't
include clean-up.

It's reassuring to know that, even if I hadn't been born her daughter, I would have been happy to have my mother as a friend.

You are here, Mother,
and you are Dead, and
here is your gift: my life
which is my home.

—Muriel Rukeyser

I'm already feeling the whole
issue of letting go of a child.
Letting go of a child in the way
that one also lets go of a
book — the tremendous exhilaration
of having completed something,
and the terrible sense of loss
that nothing else can fill.

—Mary Morris

They don't mean everything
they do and say. They are just
testing.... Take a good deal of your
daughter's behavior with a grain of
salt. Try to handle the really
outrageous as matter-of-factly
as you would a mistake in
grammar or spelling.

—Stella Chess

MOTHERS
AND DAUGHTERS

I think that as my kids get older,
they become my closest friends...
the pleasure of creativity is something
I've been able to share with my
children ever since their infancy.

—Sarah Charlesworth

My daughter thinks it's a really stupid question that I would say, "Do you feel I've neglected you for my work? Do you think I shouldn't have worked so hard?" She just thinks that's such a boring ridiculous question that it's not answerable.

—Mary Gordon

My mother always made my clothes when I was growing up. I was exacting and she was talented. My best dressed years were between the ages of six and eighteen, and it's been downhill ever since.

I love my mom's wit. I thought she talked circles around my friend's moms, and I basked silently in reflected glory.

I didn't realize the enormous, almost centrifugal force that my daughter would have for me... I was just enormously pulled into her and really didn't want to do anything else.

—Cristina Garcia

The death of my mother permanently affects my happiness, more even than I should have anticipated.... I did not apprehend, during her life, to what a degree she prevented me from feeling heart-solitude.

—Sara Coleridge

Let me not forget that I am the daughter of a woman... who herself never ceased to flower, untiringly, during three quarters of a century.

—Colette

For the mother is and must be, whether she knows it or not, the greatest, strongest and most lasting teacher her children have.

—Hannah Whitall Smith

My mother had the
power to turn an
ordinary moment into
something sweet and
subtle. The memories
I treasure most are
of things so small,
even she doesn't
remember them.

What a tremendous gift it is to be the mother of a young girl who still thinks I am perfect. I know it won't last long, but right now I am the center of her universe, and I can do no wrong. I can almost believe it myself.

MOTHERS
AND DAUGHTERS

Most mothers are instinctive philosophers.

—Harriet Beecher Stowe

I grow old, old
without you, Mother, landscape
of my heart.

—Olga Broumas

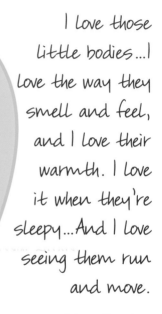

I love those little bodies...I love the way they smell and feel, and I love their warmth. I love it when they're sleepy...And I love seeing them run and move.

—Mary Gordon

Nobody made parties like
my mom. When I was eleven,
the theme was a fairy tale
complete with castle (the cake)
and dragon (hand-knit
and stuffed) woven into an
elaborate treasure hunt.
My friends were enchanted,
and I knew what it was
to be a princess.

We cooked, cleaned, labored, worried, planned, we wept and laughed, we groaned and we sang—but we never despaired.

—Kathleen Norris

I've found, as the mother of two daughters, that the love I feel for them fills me with my best self.

—Alexandra Stoddard

Love is a context,
not a behavior.

—Marilyn Ferguson

Ah, the lucky girls who grew up in the shelter of a mother's love—a mother who knows how to contrive opportunities without conceding favors, how to take advantage of propinquity without allowing appetite to be dulled by habit.

—Edith Wharton

I'll never forget how
seriously mom took me when
I explained I was thinking of
being a ballerina when I grew
up. I didn't become a ballerina,
but I learned to dance—a joy
I might have missed if she
had made me feel foolish.

MOTHERS AND DAUGHTERS

I was shocked and delighted
by my daughter's frankness. I
learned early in her life that she
could always be counted on
for an honest opinion.

When a child enters
the world through you,
it alters everything on a
psychic, psychological and
purely practical level.

—Jane Fonda

I look for ways
to spend time with my
pre-teen daughter —
walking, shopping,
taking dance classes. I
think if we're active
together now, maybe it
will stick for life.

My mother always made me feel
like a genius. It helped that I considered
her a genius — so why shouldn't
it run in the family?

Being a mother, as far as I can tell, is a constantly evolving process of adapting to the needs of your child while also changing and growing as a person in your own right.

—Deborah Insel

...everything I did you encouraged.
I cannot remember once in my
life when you were not interested
in what I was working on, or ever
suggested that I should put it
aside for something else.

—Edna St. Vincent Millay

The word "Mother" conjures up cozy visions of homespun family life: mother baking cookies, mother sympathetically listening to your tragedies, mother as your champion.

—Victoria Secunda

Mother was one of those strong, restful, yet widely sympathetic natures, in whom all around seemed to find comfort and repose.

—Harriet Beecher Stowe

Maternal women have a depth of love and emotion, a fierce protective instinct, a sense of right and wrong, and a persistence that, when used outside the home, can change the world.

—Jacqueline Hornor Plumez

I'll never forget
the first time
my daughter
laughed at one
of my jokes—
it was like
winning an Oscar.

MOTHERS
AND DAUGHTERS

I know I take my
mother for granted.
I simply can't imagine the
world without her in it.

Our children give us the opportunity
to become the parents we always
wished we'd had.

—Louise Hart

Good news and bad.
I learned my
mother's house-
keeping skills,
which means the
kids, animals,
meals, books,
play—just about
anything—come before
keeping the house neat.

It isn't easy to see the formerly loving child who once curled up in our laps turn into a surly stranger who cannot spare us a kind word. One mother...was taken aback when she called, as her daughter was going out the door, "Have a good time," and her daughter angrily replied, "Stop telling me what to do!"

—Nancy Samalin

Many daughters
have done
virtuously, but
thou excellest
them all.

—Proverbs 31:29

My daughter gives
me pinch pots, and
popsicle stick
sculptures, and
finger-painted art.
Each one gets
displayed—my
house is overflowing.

What a mother is
saying to her child with
that touch is "Live."

—Dr. Rachel Naomi Remen

Knowing that I have to stand back and let her make many of the same mistakes that I made is very painful...she'll make some that I was convinced I was going to be able to prevent a daughter from making.

—Mary Gordon

It wasn't until my daughter was born that I realized how far I had come from the innocence and joy of childhood. She opens her eyes on each new day and smiles, and I am transported back to a time when every morning was miraculous.

MOTHERS
AND DAUGHTERS

The walks and talks we have
with our two-year-olds in
red boots have a great deal to
do with the values they will
cherish as adults.

—Edith F. Hunter

I never cease to be amazed
at my daughter's sweetness
of temperament, delicacy of
feeling and perceptiveness
of mind. Are all children
so magical?

Exploring nature
with your child
is largely a
matter of
becoming receptive
to what lies
around you.

—Rachel Carson

A daughter and a goodly babe,
lusty and like to live: the queen
receives much comfort in't.

—William Shakespeare

There is nothing more
thrilling in this world, I
think, than having a child
that is yours, and yet is
mysteriously a stranger.

—Agatha Christie